The Story of a Special Day
Volume 7

January
7

January 7 is the seventh day of the year. There are 358 days remaining (359 in leap years) until the end of the year.

by Michael Dobson

Timespinner
Press

This book is also available in e-book form for Kindle, e-pub devices, and other formats from your favorite online booksellers.

For more information about the series, about us, or about your special day, please email us at editor@timespinnerpress.com.

Look for other volumes in *The Story of a Special Day,* coming often. See www.timespinnerpress.com for details and for the most recent information.

Table of Contents

For the definition of "O.S.," "N.S.," "CE," and "BCE" used with some dates , see the section "On Names and Dates."

Quote of the Day

"I do not feel obliged to believe that the same God who has endowed us with senses, reason, and intellect has intended us to forgo their use and by some other means to give us knowledge which we can attain by them."

Galileo Galilei, scientist
discovered the moons of Jupiter on January 7, 1610

Today
in
History

January 7

"Galileo Galilei showing the Doge of Venice how to use the telescope," by Giuseppe Bertini (1858)

Galileo Discovers the Moons of Jupiter

On the night of January 7, 1610, Galileo Galilei made a discovery that would revolutionize astronomy. Until that moment, it was believed that all heavenly bodies circled the earth. On that night, Galileo proved that belief false by discovering that the planet Jupiter had moons, just like the Earth.

Galileo's Telescope

The telescope was invented in the Netherlands around 1608 CE, but it was Italian scientist Galileo Galilei who first used them to study the heavens. After learning of their existence the following year, Galileo immediately set out to build one for himself, ten times more powerful than any previously built, and soon he was recording his first astronomical observations. He would make many discoveries: that supernovas were actually distant stars, that Venus had phases like the Moon, and that Saturn had rings.

About an hour after sunset on the night of January 7, 1610, Galileo trained his telescope on the planet Jupiter, and noticed three "stars" next to the planet. Unlike any other stars in the heavens, these unusually bright objects lined up almost precisely with the planet! The next night, he checked again. Now, the little "stars" were closer together. On the third night, clouds obscured his view, but on the fourth night it was clear that they had moved, one of them behind the planet itself. They weren't stars at all, but rather moons — the first discovery that other planets had moons.

Within a few weeks, Galileo discovered a fourth moon, and with that discovery confirmed that the Copernican "sun-centered" view of the Solar System was correct, a view roundly dismissed by many eminent scholars at the time.

Siderius Nuncius

That March, Galileo published a scientific pamphlet, *Siderius Nuncius,* detailing his observations. Only a few copies are known to exist, and have sold for over US $600,000 at auction. Written in Latin, it is a short book, only about 10,000 words, but contains more than 70 illustrations by Galileo himself.

He writes, "I therefore concluded...that there are three stars in the heavens moving about Jupiter, as Venus and Mercury round the Sun.... These observations also established that there are not only three, but four, erratic sidereal bodies performing their revolutions round Jupiter...the revolutions are so swift that an observer may generally get differences of position every hour."

The publication of *Siderius Nuncius* caused widespread controversy. Although we today accept the reality that the Earth is not the physical center of the universe, it came as a huge shock to many.

SIDEREVS
NVNCIVS
MAGNA, LONGEQVE ADMIRABILIA
Spectacula pandens, suspiciendaque proponens
vnicuique, præsertim verò

PHILOSOPHIS, atg *ASTRONOMIS, quæ à*

GALILEO GALILEO
PATRITIO FLORENTINO
Patauini Gymnasij Publico Mathematico

PERSPICILLI
Nuper à se reperti beneficio sunt obseruata in LVNÆ FACIE, FIXIS IN-
NVMERIS, LACTEO CIRCVLO, STELLIS NEBVLOSIS,
Apprime verò in

QVATVOR PLANETIS
Circa IOVIS Stellam disparibus interuallis, atque periodis, celeri-
tate mirabili circumuolutis; quos, nemini in hanc vsque
diem cognitos, nouissimè Author depræ-
hendit primus; atque

MEDICEA SIDERA
NVNCVPANDOS DECREVIT.

VENETIIS, Apud Thomam Baglionum. M DC X.
Superiorum Permissu, & Priuilegio.

The title page from *Siderius Nuncius* (1857)

On the one hand, poems were written expressing love for the new astronomy. Paintings were inspired by it. *Heliocentrism,* the Copernican belief that the Solar System revolved around the Sun, gained popularity.

But the negative response was also great. Galileo's claims contradicted the Biblical claim that "the world is firmly established, it cannot be moved." Some claimed his telescope was defective, and that those points of light didn't actually exist. There were scientific objections by such luminaries as Tycho Brahe as well. Strangely, many of the skeptics refused to look through the telescope themselves.

Inquisition

Eventually, Galileo's work was submitted to the Roman Inquisition, claiming that Galileo was trying to reinterpret the Bible. An Inquisitorial Commission corresponded with Galileo about his beliefs, but in the end ordered him to abandon any belief or opinion in favor of heliocentrism. Galileo complied, but continued his research.

When Urban VIII, a friend of Galileo's who opposed the Inquisition's decision, became pope in 1623, he urged Galileo to once again advocate his views. Unfortunately for Galileo, he used some of the Pope's own words in a way that made him look foolish, and soon Galileo was tried, convicted of heresy, and sentenced to house arrest for the remainder of his life. (It is not known whether

The Galilean moons (Courtesy NASA)

Galileo actually muttered, "It still moves," when the verdict was read.)

While under house arrest, he wrote Two New Sciences, praised by Albert Einstein and causing Galileo to be known as "the father of modern physics."

Because Galileo was a convicted heretic, he could not be buried in the basilica along with his ancestors, but some fifty years after his death, he was moved, all except for three fingers and a tooth, which went missing — except for the middle finger on Galileo's right hand, which is currently on exhibition at the Museo Galileo in Florence.

"Galileo facing the Roman Inquisition," Cristiano Banti (1857)

Legacy

Stephen Hawking stated that Galileo bears more of the responsibility for the birth of modern science than anybody else. Sir Isaac Newton's astronomical observations rested directly on Galileo's work.

The Catholic Church lifted its ban on Galileo's works in 1718, and by 1835 Church opposition to helicentrism was at an end. In 1992, Pope John Paul II issued a declaration citing the errors made by the tribunal that convicted Galileo, and his successor Pope Benedict XVI praised Galileo's contributions to astronomy.

During his imprisonment, Galileo was visited by poet John Milton. Painting by Solomon Alexander Hart, 1847. (Courtesy Wellcome Images, CC BY-SA 4.0)

"Crossing of the Strait of Dover by Blanchard and Jefferies"

What Happened on January 7?

From the creation of great works of engineering and art, to devastating wars and natural disasters, thousands of years of history have left their mark on each and every day of the year. Here are some important events that occurred on January 7. (Items with a photo or illustration are boxed.)

1785 — Jean-Pierre Blanchard and Dr. John Jeffries make the **first balloon trip across the English Channel.**

1904 — The **first radio distress signal**, "CQD" (−·−· −−·− −··) is established, but is quickly replaced by the simpler "SOS" (···−−−···).

1942 — Following the Japanese invasion of the Philippines in World War II, US forces retreat to the **Bataan Peninsula**, where they make a last stand for slightly more than three months.

1948 — In a highly publicized event, Kentucky Air National Guard pilot Thomas Mantell **crashes and dies while in pursuit of an unidentified flying object (UFO)**, later identified by Project Blue Book as a Skyhook balloon.

1954 — A joint team from IBM and Georgetown University demonstrates **automatic machine translation** between Russian and English.

1968 — The US unmanned lunar lander **Surveyor 7, sent to explore the surface of the Moon, lifts off.** It will land on the Moon on January 10 and transmit over 21,000 photographs back to Earth before losing contact on February 21.

1985 — The **first Japanese interplanetary spacecraft** and first deep space probe launched by an nation other than the US, Sakigate (さきがけ, "pioneer, pathfinder"), lifts off. It will do a flyby of Halley's Comet before contact is lost more than ten years later.

1989 — Following the death of his father, the Shōwa Emperor (Hirohito), **Prince Akihito** (明仁) ascends the Chrysanthemum Throne to become **Emperor of Japan (天皇).**

1991 — A **coup d-état in Haiti** led by Tonton Macoute leader Roger Lafontant fails, leading to his arrest.

1999 — The Senate trial in the **impeachment of US President Bill Clinton** begins; it ends in his acquittal after 21 days.

2015 — Two Islamist gunmen force their way into the Paris headquarters of *Charlie Hebdo* magazine, **killing 12 and wounding 11,** leading to an international outcry of support under the slogan *Je suis Charlie* ("I am Charlie.")

The Surveyor lunar probe (top), Tycho Crater photomosaic taken by
Surveyor 7 (bottom). (Courtesy NASA/JPL)

Quote of the Day

"An honorable defeat is better than a dishonorable victory."

Millard Fillmore, 13th US President
born January 7, 1800

Births
and
Deaths

January 7

Nikola Tesla, inventor. Tesla died January 7, 1943

Notable January 7 People

With the current world population at about seven billion people, on average about 19 million people also celebrate their birthdays on January 7 — and that isn't counting millions and millions who came before! No matter when you were born, you share your birthday with many special people whose accomplishments (and occasionally embarrassments) have been noted as part of history.

In this section, you'll meet fascinating people who share your birthday. They're organized by what they're famous for, and then in reverse chronological order from most recent to earliest. Those who are shown in photographs or artwork have a box around them. We don't have photos of everyone, so please forgive us if your favorite person is missing.

Some of these people you've heard of, others will be new to you, but they all make up an important part of the reason that January 7 is a truly special day!

The Addams Family, by cartoonist Charles Addams, from the cover
of the book *Dear Dead Days*. (© Charles Addams)

Who Was Born on January 7?

Achievement

Valeri Kubasov (Вале́рий Куба́сов), cosmonaut on three space missions, including the Apollo-Soyuz million, first person to weld in space. *(1935)*

Evelyn "Bobbi" Trout, pioneering female aviator and record-setter, nicknamed for her short "bob" haircut. *(1906)*

William Clarence Matthews, African-American pioneer in politics, law, and sports; standout baseball player at Harvard; only African-American player in a white professional baseball league in 1905; became an attorney, serving as US Assistant Attorney General in the Coolidge administration. *(1877)*

Art and Illustration

Charles Addams, cartoonist known for dark humor, creator of The Addams Family. *(1912)*

Business and Technology

Sir Hudson Fysh, Australian aviator who co-founded the airline Qantas. *(1895)*

Thomas Henry Ismay, founded the White Star Line, owner of RMS *Titanic*. His son Joseph survived the sinking of that ship. *(1837)*

Heinrich von Stephan, German postmaster who helped found the Universal Postal Union, which created the worldwide postal system. *(1831)*

Sir Sandford Fleming, Canadian railway engineer and inventor, credited with originating the concept of Universal Standard Time. *(1827)*

Journalism and Letters

Katie Couric, television journalist best known as co-host of *The Today Show* and anchor of the *CBS Evening News*, member of the Television Hall of Fame. *(1957)*

Jann Wenner, co-founded and published *Rolling Stone* magazine; member of the Rock and Roll Hall of Fame. *(1946)*

William Peter Blatty, writer and filmmaker best known for his novel and screenplay for the *The Exorcist*. *(1928)*

Gerald Durrell, naturalist and zookeeper known for his books and television programs on animals; brother of novelist Lawrence Durrell. *(1925)*

Katie Couric (Photo: David Shankbone, CC BY-SA 3.0)

Military and Government

Rand Paul, US Senator and conservative presidential candidate. *(1963)*

Orval Faubus, Arkansas governor best remembered for ordering the National Guard to prevent black students from attending Little Rock Central High School. *(1910)*

Millard Fillmore, 13th US President, became president on the death of his predecessor Zachary Taylor. *(1800)*

Joseph Bonaparte, elder brother of Napoléon Bonaparte; King of Naples, Sicily, and Spain during his brother's reign as emperor. *(1768)*

Israel Putnam, American general during the Revolutionary War, known for his exploits at the Battle of Bunker Hill. *(1502)*

Music and Dance

Kathy Valentine, guitar and bass player best known as a member of The Go-Gos. (1959)

Juan Gabriel, Mexican singer-songwriter whose albums have sold over 100 million copies worldwide. *(1950)*

Kenny Loggins, singer-songwriter best known for his partnership with Kenny Loggins as Loggins and Messina, nominated for an Academy Award for his song "Footloose." *(1948)*

Millard Fillmore (Photo: Mathew Brady)

Vera de Bossett (Stravinsky), by Serge Soudeikine

Tommy Johnson, orchestral tuba player best known for playing the shark theme from the film *Jaws.* *(1935)*

Jean-Pierre Rampal, French flautist who made the flute a popular solo instrument for classical music again. *(1922)*

Eric Jupp, known to Australian audiences for his theme music to the TV show *Skippy the Bush Kangaroo.* (1922)

Red Allen, well known jazz trumpeter and vocalist whose career spanned more than 40 years. *(1908)*

Vera de Bosset, dancer and artist best known as the mistress and later second wife of composer Igor Stravinsky. *(1873)*

Performing Arts

Jeremy Renner, actor known for his roles in *The Hurt Locker, The Bourne Legacy,* and as Hawkeye in the Marvel film franchise. (1971)

Doug E. Doug, comedian and actor known for his roles on the sitcom *Cosby* and for the film *Cool Runnings.* *(1970)*

Nicholas Cage, actor known for such films as *Raising Arizona, Moonstruck,* and *Con Air;* received an Academy Award for his performance in *Leaving Las Vegas.* *(1964)*

Butterfly McQueen in *Gone With the Wind*

David Caruso, actor best known for his roles in the TV series *NYPD Blue* and *CSI: Miami. (1956)*

Sammo Hung (洪金寶), Hong Kong actor and martial artist who appeared in such films as *Enter the Dragon, Game of Death,* and various Jackie Chan films. *(1952)*

Terry Moore, actress nominated for an Academy Award for 1952's *Come Back Little Sheba. (1929)*

Gene L. Coon, screenwriter and television producer best known for his work on the original *Star Trek. (1924)*

Vincent Gardenia, actor nominated for the Academy Award for his roles in *Bang the Drum Slowly* and *Moonstruck. (1920)*

Butterfly McQueen, actress best known as Scarlett O'Hara's maid in the 1939 film *Gone With the Wind. (1911)*

Alan Napier, British stage and screen actor best known to American audiences as Alfred the butler in the 1960s television series *Batman. (1873)*

Adolph Zukor, film producer who founded and ran Paramount Pictures. *(1873)*

Religion

Eliezer Ben-Yehuda (אליעזר בן־יהודה), considered the driving spirit behind the revival of Hebrew in the modern era. *(1858)*

Pope Gregory XIII, Catholic pontiff best remembered for commissioning the modern Gregorian calendar.* *(1502)*

Science

Sir John Walker, received the 1997 Nobel Prize in Chemistry for his work in molecular biology. *(1941)*

Sports

Vasily Alekseyev (Василий Алексеев), Soviet weightlifter who set 80 world records and won two Olympic gold medals, called the "World's Strongest Man" by *Sports Illustrated. (1942)*

Manfred Schellscheidt, German-American soccer coach and player, member of the National Soccer Hall of Fame. *(1941)*

Charlie Jenkins, American runner who won two gold medals in track at the 1956 Olympic Games. *(1934)*

---

* To learn more about the different calendar types, see "What Day of the Week is January 7?"

Eddie LeBaron, member of the College Football Hall of Fame for his time with the College of the Pacific; played professionally for the Washington Redskins and Dallas Cowboys. *(1930)*

Johnny Mize, first baseman for the Cardinals, the Giants, and the Yankees, member of the Baseball Hall of Fame. *(1913)*

Thomas Hicks, marathon runner who won the gold medal at the 1904 Olympics. *(1858)*

Vasily Alekseyev

Shōwa Emperor (Hirohito) at his coronation in 1928

Who Died on January 7?

Government and Politics

Shōwa Emperor (昭和天皇), better known to Americans as Hirohito (reigning Japanese emperors do not have a personal name), 124th Emperor of Japan. *(1989)*

Lou Henry Hoover, First Lady of the United States in the administration of her husband, Herbert Hoover. *(1944)*

Sir Edmund Barton, politician and judge who served as the first Prime Minister of Australia. *(1920)*

Catherine of Aragon, first wife of English King Henry VIII. *(1536)*

Journalism and Letters

P. D. Eastman, children's book author and illustrator whose best-known works include *Are You My Mother?* and *Go, Dog, Go!* *(1986)*

Alvar Lidell, BBC radio announcer and newsreader particularly popular during the Second World War. *(1981)*

John Berryman, influential American poet. *(1972)*

Edward Channing, historian who won the Pulitzer Prize for History for his six-volume *History of the United States,* which has become a standard reference work for scholars. *(1931)*

Military and Adventure

Heinrich Harrer, mountaineer best known for his 1952 book *Seven Years in Tibet,* basis for a 1956 and 1997 film of the same name. *(2006)*

Osa Helen Johnson, adventuress and documentary filmmaker with her partner and husband Martin Johnson, wrote the bestselling 1940 book *I Married Adventure. (1953)*

André Maginot, French Minister of War who advocated a string of defensive forts that became known as the Maginot Line, which was unsuccessful in stopping the German invasion in World War II. *(1932)*

Music

Troy Shondell, American rock singer and one-hit wonder (for "This Time") who inspired Tommy James to name his group The Shon-dells in his honor. *(2016)*

Kitty Kallen, singer in the swing and big band era, best known for her 1954 recording of "Little Things Mean a Lot." *(2016)*

Kitty Kallen (left) with Doris Day (Photo: William P. Gottlieb)

Larry Williams, American rock and blues singer-songwriter whose hits included "Bony Moronie" and "Dizzy Miss Lizzy." *(1980)*

Performing Arts

Rod Taylor, actor who appeared in more than 50 films, including *The Birds, The Time Machine,* and *Inglourious Basterds. (2015)*

Sir Run Run Shaw (邵逸夫), founded the leading television company and one of the largest film production studios in Hong Kong. *(2014)*

Avery Schreiber, comedian and actor remembered as part of the act Burns and Schreiber with Jack Burns. *(2002)*

Trevor Howard, actor particularly known for his roles in the films *Brief Encounter* and *The Third Man. (1988)*

Science

Vladimir Prelog, received the 1975 Nobel Prize in Chemistry for his research into the stereochemistry of organic molecules and reactions. *(1998)*

Alfred Kastler, French physicist who won the 1966 Nobel Prize for developing the technique of "optical pumping," critical in the later development of the laser. *(1984)*

Nikola Tesla, scientist and inventor important in the development of the electrical supply system, known as a futurist and visionary. *(1943) (Photo page 14)*

Sports

Bronko Nagurski, NFL tackle and fullback primarily known for his years with the Chicago Bears, member of the Pro Football Hall of Fame; also a multiple-time World Heavyweight Champion wrestler. *(1990)*

Dorothea Lambert Chambers, British tennis player who won seven Wimbledon titles and an Olympic gold medal. *(1943)*

Dorothea Lambert Chambers

Quote of the Day

"Within a few years a simple and inexpensive device, readily carried about, will enable one to receive on land or sea the principal news, to hear a speech, a lecture, a song or play of a musical instrument, conveyed from any other region of the globe."

Nikola Tesla, inventor
died January 7, 1943

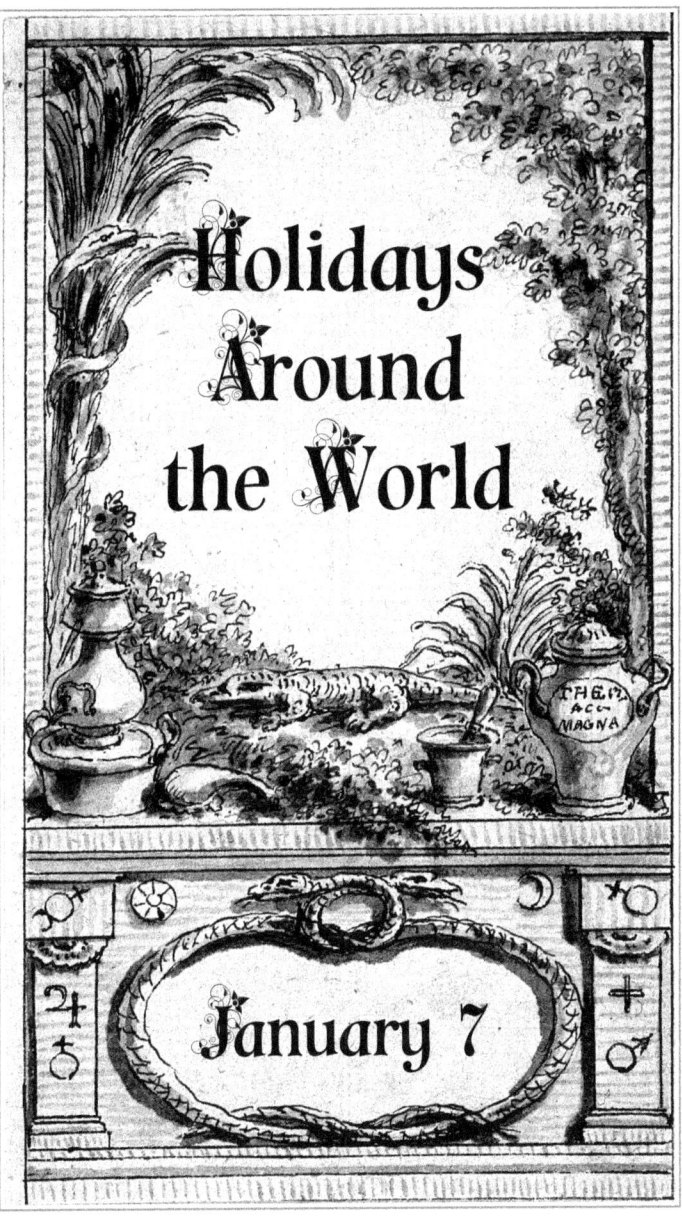

Holidays
Around
the World

January 7

Orthodox Christmas in Belarus, with Grandfather Frost

Holidays Around the World

If you're looking for a reason to take your special day off, you should know that every single day is a holiday somewhere in the world! Here's some of what you can celebrate on January 7!

Christmas

Don't pack up those Christmas decorations just yet, because January 7 is Christmas Day in the Eastern and Oriental Orthodox Churches, which use the older Julian[†] calendar. According to that older calendar, January 7 *is* December 25!

Rastafarians also celebrate Christmas on January 7, because their traditions derive from the Ethiopian Orthodox Church, which follows the Orthdox calendar.

General Events

Distaff Day (many European Catholic countries)

In medieval times, January 7, the day after the Feast of the Epiphany, was known as Distaff Day (or St. Distaff Day), in which women resumed their

---

[†] To learn more about the different calendar types, see "What Day of the Week is January 7?"

household work after the end of the Twelve Days of Christmas on January 5.

Festa de Tricolore (Italy)

Many nations have a day to celebrate their national flag. In Italy, the tricolor Italian flag is honored on January 7.

Nanakusa no Sekku (七草の節句) (Japan)

On January 7, the Japanese celebrate the Festival of Seven Herbs (*Nanakusa no sekku*), eating seven-herb rice porridge.

Pioneer's Day (Liberia)

January 7 in Liberia commemorates the arrival of the first Americo-Liberians in 1820. It is controversial in that country because of historical tensions between Anglo-Liberians and indigenous Liberians.

Victory Day/Victory from Genocide Day (Cambodia)

In Cambodia, January 7 is a national holiday commemorating the end of the Khmer Rouge regime.

Food Holidays

In the United States, almost every day of the year is dedicated to a particular food. (Some other countries also have official food days, but only in America is there one every single day!) Sponsored by manufacturers, retailers, farmers, or simply fans, these days are often proclaimed by the President, Congress, state governors, or mayors. Given that there are more different foods than days of the year, some days honor more than one kind of food!

In the US, January 7 is **National Tempura Day.** Although tempura is known as a Japanese dish, according to Foodimentary it was originally introduced to Japan in the mid-sixteenth century. Even the name, "tempura," is derived from the Latin "tempora."

In addition, the entire month of January is used to celebrate numerous foods.

- California Dried Plum Digestive Health Month
- Fat Free Living Month
- National Hot Tea Month
- National Oatmeal Month
- National Slow Cooking Month
- National Soup Month
- National Baking Month
- National Fat Free Living Month

And while we're on the subject of food, January is also **Weight Loss Awareness Month**, in case you've already forgotten those New Year's resolutions.

Religious Feast Days and Holidays

Each day in the year is considered a feast day for one or more saints. They are somewhat different in western Christianity (Catholicism and many forms of Protestantism) and in eastern (Orthodox)

Christianity. There are many others; this is a selection.

In *Western Christianity*, January 7 is the feast day for Saint André Bessette, Canute Lavard, Charles of Sezze, Lucian of Antioch, and Raymond of Peñafort.

In *Eastern Orthodox Christianity*, it is also the commemoration of Saints Julian the Deacon, Crispin of Pavia, Valentine of Rhaetia, Brannock of Braunton, Cedd, Cronan Beg, Tillo of Solignac, Kentigerna, Emilian, Aldric of Le Mans, Reinold, Anastatius of Sens, and Fedor I of Russia. (These people are honored on December 25 by "Old Calendrists.")

Honorary Months

Presidents, Congresses, and nations around the world issue proclamations recognizing particular months to honor certain causes. These events generally fall in January, though honorary months do come and go. Holidays established by states and nonprofit organizations are listed if verified. If not otherwise specified, all months are US. There is some variation from year to year; some celebratory months get added and others get dropped. Two places to get up to date information are the current edition of *Chase's Calendar of Events* or the website Brownielocks. Here are some honorary designations for January.

- Adopt a Rescued Bird Month
- Bath Safety Month
- Be Kind to Food Servers Month
- Birth Defects Month

- California Dried Plum Digestive Month
- Cervical Health Awareness Month
- Financial Wellness Month
- Get Organized Month
- International Child-Centered Divorce Awareness Month
- International Creativity Month
- National Braille Literacy Month

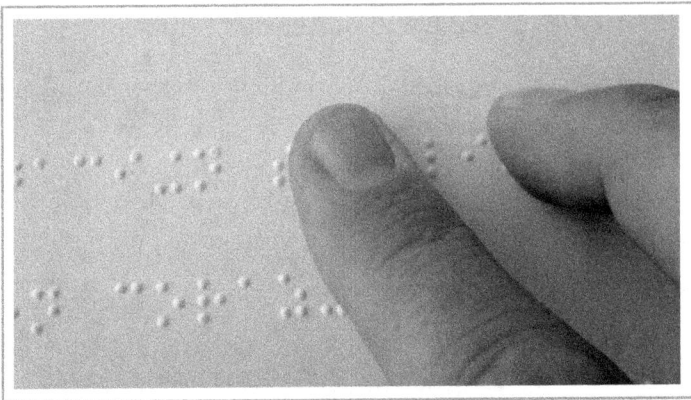

A person reading a braille book, for National Braille Literacy Month
(Photo: Antonio X Alonso CC BY-SA 2.0)

- National Clean Up Your Computer Month
- National Codependency Awareness Month
- National Mentoring Month
- National Polka Music Month
- National Poverty in America Awareness Month
- National Skating Month

- National Thank You Month
- National Volunteer Blood Donor Month
- Slavery and Human Trafficking Prevention Month
- Stalking Awareness Month
- Teen Driving Awareness Month
- Train Your Dog Month (also Walk Your Dog Month)

Moveable and Multi-Day Events

Some events take place over a specific week or time period. Start and finish dates may vary from year to year. Some events occur on different days each year (such as "fourth Saturday of a month"). These events sometimes take place on or include January 7.

First Week of January

- Celebration of Life Week
- Diet Resolution Week
- Silent Record Week
- New Year's Resolution Week

Week Long Celebrations that Sometimes Include January 7

- Home Office Safety and Security Week
- National Lose Weight/Feel Great Week
- Elvis's Birthday Celebration Week (week that includes Elvis's birthday, January 8)

1st Friday (can be any day between January 1-7)

- Children's Day (Bahamas)

1st Monday (can be any day between January 1-7)

- Handsel Monday (Scotland and northern England)

Monday after Epiphany (January 7-13)

- Plough Monday, in medieval times the day men returned to work following the end of the Twelve Days of Christmas.

A Plough Monday celebration in Yorkshire (1814)

Non-Gregorian Events

Not every culture uses the familiar Gregorian calendar, so some events not only shift within a range of a few days depending on the year, but may even migrate through the months. Here is a selection of events around the world that sometimes take place on January 7.

- Dhanurmas (Hindu calendar)
- Thiruvathira (Hinduism, Tamil calendar)
- Lohri (Punjab)
- Thai Pongal (Hinduism, Tamil calendar)
- Mattu Pongal (Hinduism, Tamil calendar)
- Makara Sankranthi (Hinduism)
- Thaipusam (Hinduism, Tamil calendar)
- Tu B'Shevat

Just For Fun

Anyone can make up a holiday, and many people do! These holidays are unofficial, and some of them come and go, but here are a few more reasons to celebrate on January 7!

- Fruitcake Toss Day (first Saturday, January 1-7)
- Harlem Globetrotters Day
- I'm Not Going to Take It Any More Day
- National Bobblehead Day

January, by Eugène Grasset

Quote of the Day

"It's easy to kill a movie. Just move it to January."

Mike Myers, as "Dr. Evil"
from the *Austin Powers* movies

About
the
Month
of

THE
ACC—
MAGNA

January

"January," from the *Brevarium Grimani* by Simon Bening (c.1510)

January: The First Month

That blasts of January
Would blow you through and through.
— *William Shakespeare*, The Winter's Tale

January wasn't always the first month in the year. In ancient Rome, March was the first month until about 450 BCE. Even after January became the official first month in the calendar, Romans still counted dates from the inauguration of the consuls, March 15 and May 1.

In the Middle Ages, Christian feast days were used to start the new year, including March 25 and December 25. It wasn't until the 16th century that European nations made January 1 the official start of the new year. (This was called "Circumcision Style" because January 1 was also celebrated as the Feast of the Circumcision of Jesus.)

The name January (*Ianuarius*) is derived from the Roman god Janus, the god of beginning and transitions. Janus gives his name to the Latin word for door (*ianua*), because January is the door to the year. Janus is normally portrayed as having two faces, one looking toward the future and one toward the past. In spite of that, the goddess Juno was the patron of that month.

In both the Julian and Gregorian calendars‡, January is the first month of the year and one of seven months with 31 days. In the Northern Hemisphere, January is the coldest month of the year, and in the Southern Hemisphere, it's the warmest, equivalent to the Northern Hemisphere's July.

January in Other Cultures

The month of January has different names in different languages. Some nations use calendars other than the Gregorian, and their months may overlap with January. In lunar-based calendars, such as the Islamic calendar, months move through the seasons. Still, many languages often have a word for January itself.

Albanian: Janar

Anglo-Saxon: Wulf-monath

Arabic (Egypt, Sudan, Yemen): يوناأغيناير (*yanāyir*)

Arabic (Levant): حزيركانون الثاني (*kānūn al-thānī*)

Arabic (Libya): الصهنار (*aynu n-nār*)

Arabic (Algeria and Tunisia): جأينجانفي (*Jānfī*)

Arabic (Morocco): غيناير (*yanāyər*)

Azerbaijani: Yanvar

Basque: Urtarril

Bulgarian: януари (*januari*)

---

‡ To learn more about the different calendar types, see "What Day of the Week is January 7?"

Chinese: 一月 (Cantonese: *yātyuht*; Mandarin: *yīyuè*; Taiwanese: *it-goeh*)
Corsican: Ghjennaghju
Croatian: Siječanj
Czech: Leden
Finnish: Tammikuu (oak moon)
French: Janvier
German/Danish/Norwegian/Slovenian: Januar
Greek: Ιανουάριος (*Ianouários*)
Haitian Creole: Janvye
Hebrew: ינואר (*yanû'ar*)
Hindi: जनवरी (*janvarī*)
Hungarian: Január
Irish (Gaelic): Eanáir mí Eanáir
Italian: Gennaio
Japanese: 一月 (*ichigatsu*), 睦月 (*mutsuki*)
Kazakh: Қаңтар (*Ķaņtar*)
Korean: 일월 (*ilweol*)
Lithuanian: Sausis
Maori: Kohitātea
Old English: Se æfterra Gēola
Polish: Styczeń
Portuguese: Janeiro
Russian: январь (*janvar'*)
Scottish Gaelic: am Faoilleach
Sesotho: Pherekgong
Slovene: Prosinec
Spanish: Enero

Swahili/Dutch/Swedish: Januari
Swazi: Bhimbidvwane
Thai: มกราคม (*makarakhom*)
Turkish: Ocak
Vietnamese: 腩爻 (*tháng một*)
Walloon: Djanvî
Welsh: Ionawr
Yiddish: אויגויאַנואַר (*yanuar*)
Zulu: uJanuwari

Mengapa?   Zašto?
      Por quê?   Чаму?   为什么呢？
                        Чому?
Poukisa?   کیوں؟   Per què?
   Tại sao?   Miks?
            Bakit?   Kial?   ?למה
     Waarom?   Hvers vegna?
どうして？   פֿאַרוואָס?   Niyə?
Warum?   Dlaczego?   Pourquoi?
Ինչու́?   چرا؟   Quid?
  Cén fáth?   Зашто?   Pam?
   Zergatik?   რატომ?
Kwa nini?   Proč?   Miért?
  De ce?   Hoekom?
             Kodėl?   क्यों?
    เพราะเหตุใด   Защо?   Why?
Perché?   Miksi?
   لماذا؟   Prečo?   Varför?
          Γιατί;
Għaliex?   ¿Por qué?   Pse?
  왜?   Почему?
  Kāpēc?   Neden?   Зошто?
    Hvorfor?   為什麼呢？

January Sayings and Superstitions

Here are some sayings and superstitions associated with the month of January.

New Year Superstitions

- It's important to kiss those dearest to us at the stroke of the New Year to keep their affections for the next twelve months.

- The new year must not be seen with bare cupboards. Stock up on supplies and make sure there's plenty of money in ever wallet in the home.

- Do not begin the new year with the household in debt.

- The first person to enter your home after the stroke of midnight will tell you the kind of year you will have.

- Do not let anything leave your house on the first day of the year, not even garbage.

- Start your year off with good luck by eating hoppin' john, a dish made with black-eyed peas and rice (southern United States).

- Wear something new on January 1.

- Be sure to open the door at midnight to let the old year escape.

- Babies born on New Year's Day will always have good luck.

January Wedding Superstitions

- A January bride will be a prudent housekeeper, and very good tempered.

- Married in January's hoar and rime / Widowed you'll be before your prime.

- Married when the year is new, he'll be loving, kind and true.

January Symbols

Birthstone: Garnet, representing constancy.

Soviet postage stamp showing a geologist finding garnets

Birth Flower (Britain): Carnation, representing love, fascination, and distinction

Vase with Red and White Carnation on a Yellow Background,
by Vincent van Gogh

Birth Flower (America): Carnation or Snowdrop (*Galanthus*)

A New Year's greeting card with snowdrops

Birth Flower (China): Plum blossom (*prunus mume*)

Red Plum Blossom (Photo: Frank Gualtieri)

Birth Flower (Japan): Camellia

Camellias (Clara Maria Pope)

Michael Dobson

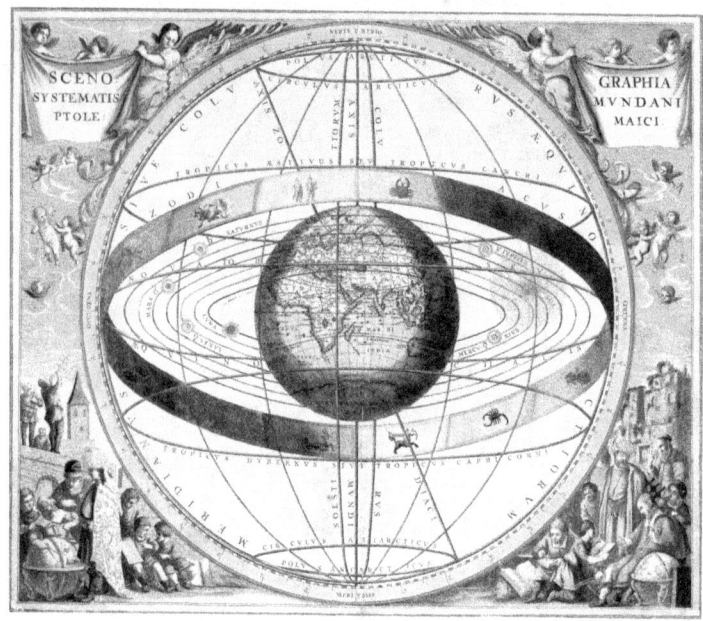

Scenography of the Ptolemaic Cosmography, by Johannes van Loon, based on Andreas Cellarius's *Harmonia Macrocosmica,* 1660

January 7 Zodiac Signs

From the perspective of someone on Earth, the Sun appears to move through the sky throughout the year, along a path astronomers call the *ecliptic plane*. The ecliptic plane is divided into twelve constellations, known as the zodiac, based on traditionally observed patterns of stars. On your birthday, you can't see your constellation, because it's in the daytime sky.

The zodiac was first developed by Babylonian astronomers about 2,500 years ago. Because they were unaware that the Earth wobbles like a spinning top (known as *precession*), they didn't make allowance for the fact that the Sun's path through the zodiac changes over time.

That means there are now two sets of dates for your birth sign. The *tropical dates* are the original Babylonian dates; the *sidereal dates* tell you where the Sun actually appears as it moves along its annual path.

For January 7, the tropical signs is **Capricorn** and the sidereal sign is **Sagittarius**.

Capricorn

Tropical December 22 to January 20
Sidereal January 15 to February 14

The origins of the constellation Capricorn date back to Sumeria and Babylonia. Based on Enki, the Sumerian god of wisdom and waters, Capricorn has the head and upper body of a mountain goat and the lower body and tail of a fish. The mountain goat represents ambition and intelligence, the fish represents passion and spirituality.

An earth sign, Capricorn is ruled by the planet Saturn. They are often thought to be responsible, patient, ambitious and loyal, but can sometimes be seen as conceited, distrusting, and unimaginative. Capricornians are supposed to be compatible with Taurus, Pisces, and Virgo, but not with Aries, Sagittarius, or Leo.

Sagittarius

Tropical November 23 to December 21
Sidereal December 16 to January 14

The centaur (half-man, half-horse) Chiron was famous as a healer and as an archer. He tutored Achilles, Jason (of Argonaut fame), and Hercules. Unfortunately for Chiron, Hercules accidentally shot him with an arrow that had been dipped in hydra poison. He was unable to find a cure, so gave up his immortality to free Prometheus, and died. In recognition of his sacrifice, Zeus placed him among the stars.

In astrology, Sagittarians are known for their independence and craving for adventure and excitement. They are encouraging and kind, but sometimes lack commitment. They are supposed to be compatible with Aries, Leo, and Libra, but not with Taurus, Scorpio, or Capricorn.

Illustration by Edward Penfield

What Day of the Week is January 7?

On what day of the week does January 7 fall?

Surprisingly, this isn't an easy question. Because the calendar year is 365 days long (366 in leap years), it doesn't divide evenly by the seven days of the week.

Also, the Earth goes around the Sun in about 365-1/4 days, so a calendar tends to drift over time. That's why the same date falls on different weekdays in different years.

This is made even more complicated by a change in calendars that took place in 1582. Our modern calendar has its roots in ancient Rome, in a calendar reform conducted by Julius Caesar. Caesar commissioned mathematicians to attack the problem, and they came up with the idea of leap years, and thus standardized the calendar for centuries to come. This was called the Julian calendar.

Over time, however, the small errors in Caesar's calculation compounded. That's why Pope Gregory XIII commissioned the Gregorian calendar, used in most of the world today. Some countries converted in 1582, when the calendar was first developed; some converted later; other still haven't changed.

Gregorian and Julian aren't the only types of calendars. The Hebrew year, the Islamic year, and many other calendars are used in different parts of the world and among different people.

You can convert Gregorian dates to other calendars, including the Hebrew calendar, the Islamic calendar, and even the Mayan calendar by visiting the Fourmilab Calendar Converter at http://www.fourmilab.ch/documents/calendar/.

Chinese calendar systems are quite complex and have changed several times; a full discussion is far beyond the scope of this book. If you're interested, you can find information here: http://www.hermetic.ch/cal_stud/chinese_cal.htm.

On Names and Dates

Historians use "CE" (Common Era) and "BCE" (Before the Common Era) instead of the more common "AD" (Anno Domini, or Year of Our Lord) and "BC" (Before Christ), reflecting the fact that the year-numbering system established by the Gregorian calendar is used throughout the world in many countries not culturally Christian.

The CE/BCE designation dates back to at least 1708, and has been adopted as a standard by the United Nations and the Universal Postal Union. Because this series of books covers events and people of all nations and cultures, we use the CE/BCE terms.

The abbreviation "O.S." ("Old Style") on some dates refers to the fact that the Russian Empire did not switch from the Julian to the Gregorian calendar at the same time as the rest of Europe, and therefore some figures and events have two dates.

Also, in the Julian calendar in England in the 16th century, the year began on March 25 rather than January 1. To avoid confusion with Gregorian dates, dates between January and March were often written using both years.

People and events whose original names are not in the Western alphabet have their native names (where possible) in the appropriate script shown in parenthesis. If you are using an e-reader to access an electronic version of this book, all characters don't always display on all devices.

A 50-year brass perpetual calendar.

Quote of the Day

"Time is an illusion, lunchtime doubly so."

Douglas Adams,
from *The Hitchhiker's Guide to the Galaxy*

Notes and Credits

Timespinner
Press

Cartoon by John T. McCutcheon

Copyright, Credit, and Contact

Follow Us

Our blog "This Day in History" (http://
timespinnerpress.com/this-day-in-history/) features short
articles on events and people associated with each day, and
updates several times each week. Also subscribe to the
"Quote of the Day" at http://timespinnerpress.com/quote-
of-the-day/. You can get daily links by following us on
Facebook at TimespinnerPress, or on Twitter as
@sidewisethinker.

Contact Us

Find an error or a format problem? Want information about
the series, about us, or about when the volume for your
special day might be available? Please email us at
editor@timespinnerpress.com. (We also take requests if your
special day isn't yet complete. Please give us at least six
weeks' notice if possible.)

Sources

We owe a great debt to Wikipedia, which is our first stop for
research. We attempt to make independent confirmation of
all important dates and facts through a variety of other
sources.

Other sources we frequently use include the Library of
Congress; "on this day" listings from *Encyclopedia Britannica*,
the *New York Times*, and the BBC; Omniglot for the names of
months in other languages; *Chase's Calendar of Events*; and, of
course, the always essential Google.

All art and photographs are either in the public domain, used under a Creative Commons license, or with a "fair use" justification, and most frequently come from Wikimedia Commons and the Library of Congress Prints and Photographs Division.

Attribution is provided where possible, or as requested by the copyright owner, or when there is particular historical significance, listed below. For information about any particular illustration or photograph, please contact us.

Credits

1. The cover painting of Galileo Galilei was painted by an unknown artist in the 18th century, and is in the public domain because its copyright has expired. The image is from the Wellcome Images collection, ICV No. 23920, Photo V0023487, and is used here under CC BY-SA 4.0.

2. The illustration of the month of January used on the back cover is from the French Gothic illuminated manuscript *Les Très Riches Heures du duc de Berry* by the Limbourg Brothers, Jean Colombe, and an intermediate painter whose name is lost to history.

3. The box graphic used on the first page is from a 1916 pamphlet entitled "Divorce versus Democracy" authored by G. K. Chesterton, originally published in London by the Society of St. Peter and St. Paul. It is in the public domain in the US because it was published prior to 1923, and is in the public domain in all countries (including the country of origin) in which the copyright time is the author's life plus 70 years or less.

4. The graphic design for the section pages in this book is from a design originally created for a pharmacy label. It is from Wellcome Images (ICV No 11073, photo V0010813), and is used here under CC BY-SA 4.0.

5. The 1858 fresco "Galileo Galilei showing the Doge of Venice how to use the telescope" is by Giuseppe Bertini, and is in the public domain because its copyright has expired. The

fresco itself can be seen in the Bertini Room of the Villa Andrea Ponti in Varese, Italy.

6. The artwork of the Galilean moons contrasted to the size of Jupiter is in the public domain as a work created by NASA.

7. The title page from *Siderius Nuncius* by Galileo Galilei was originally published in 1610, and is in the public domain because its copyright has expired.

8. The 1857 painting "Galileo facing the Roman Inquisition" by Cristiano Banti is in the public domain because its copyright has expired.

9. The 1847 painting "Milton visiting Galileo when a prisoner of the Inquisition" by Solomon Alexander Hart is in the public domain because its copyright has expired. It is from Wellcome Images (ICV No 18220, photo L0025611), and is used here under CC BY-SA 4.0.

10. The card "N°. 7 – Traversée en ballon du Pas-de-Calais par Blanchard et Jefferies (1785)" is from a set of collectable cards picturing events in the history of ballooning and parachuting, first published between 1890 and 1900 by Romanet & cie., Paris. It is in the public domain because its copyright has expired.. The image is courtesy of the Library of Congress Prints and Pictures Division, digital ID ppmsca. 02562.

11. The NASA/JPL photographs from the Surveyor 7 mission are in the public domain as works created by NASA.

12. The 1896 photograph of Nikola Tesla is in the public domain because its copyright has expired. The photographer is unknown.

13. The cover for the book *Dear Dead Days* by Charles Addams is copyrighted by the artist and the publisher and is not in the public domain. Its use here is under the "fair use" provisions of the copyright code, because it helps identify a person of historical importance. The image is cropped, printed in black & white rather than color, and is of a smaller size and resolution than the original, and therefore not suitable for the creation of counterfeit goods. No challenge to the copyright status of this material is intended.

14. The 2012 photograph of Katie Couric was taken by David Shankbone, and is used here under CC BY-SA 3.0.

15. The Mathew Brady photograph of US President Millard Fillmore was taken between 1855 and 1865. It is in the public domain because its copyright has expired. The image is courtesy of the Library of Congress, digital ID cwpbh.00699. It has been cropped.

16. The portrait of Vera de Bosset is by Serge Soudeikine, and is from the collection of the Bibliothèque nationale de France. According to that institution, the image is in the public domain.

17. The publicity photograph of Butterfly McQueen from the 1939 film *Gone With the Wind* is in the public domain because it was first published in the US between 1923 and 1977 without a copyright notice. Traditionally, publicity photographs are not copyrighted because of the way in which they are intended to be used.

18. The photograph of weightlifter Vasily Alekseyev is in the public domain in Italy, its country of origin, because its copyright has expired according to the Law for the Protection of Copyright and Neighbouring Rights n.633, 22 April 1941 and later revisions

19. The photograph from the coronation of Prince Hirohito as Emperor was taken by the Imperial Household Agency in 1928. It is in the public domain in its country of origin under Japanese copyright law.

20. The photograph of Doris Day and Kitty Kallen in Central Park was taken by William P. Gottlieb in 1947, and is part of the William P. Gottlieb Collection at the Library of Congress (LC-GLB13-0185). In accordance with the wishes of Gottlieb, the photographs in his collection entered into the public domain on February 16, 2010.

21. The photograph of Dorothea Douglass Lambert Chambers originally appeared in the 1908 book *The Complete Lawn Tennis Player* by A. W. Myers (George W. Jacobs & Co., Philadelphia). It is in the public domain because its copyright has expired. The name of the photographer is unknown.

22. The 2009 photograph of Grandfather Frost in Belarus was taken by Paju, and is used here under CC BY-SA 3.0.

23. The photograph of a person reading a braille book was taken by Antonio X. Alonso in 2009. It is used here under CC BY-SA 2.0.

24. The drawing of a Plough Monday celebration was taken from George Walker's 1814 book *The Costumes of Yorkshire*. It is in the public domain because its copyright has expired.

25. The 1896 postcard "January" by Eugène Grasset is in the public domain because its copyright has expired.

26. The 1815 woodcut of a Regency era wedding proposal is in the public domain because its copyright has expired.

27. The painting *January* is from the *Brevarium Gremani,* circa 1510, and is in the public domain because its copyright has expired.

28. The graphic of "Why" in several languages was created in 2011 by "Maierstrahl," and is used here under CC BY-SA 3.0.

29. The 1968 USSR postage stamp "Prospecting Geologist with Found Diamond and Red Crystals-Pyropes (Garnets)" is not an object of copyright according to Part IV of Civil Code No. 230-FZ of the Russian Federation (2006).

30. The 1886 painting "Vase with Red and White Carnations on a Yellow Background" by Vincent Van Gogh is in the public domain because its copyright has expired.

31. The German New Year's greeting card was made circa 1900. It is in the public domain because its copyright has expired.

32. The 2006 photograph of a red plum blossom (*prunus mume*) was taken by Frank Gualtieri, who released the photograph into the public domain.

33. The illustration of camellias by Clara Maria Pope is from Samuel Curtis' *Monograph on the Genus Camellia*, published in 1819. It is in the public domain because its copyright has expired.

34. The celestial sphere is from *Scenography of the Ptolemaic Cosmography*, by Johannes van Loon, based on Andreas Cellarius's *Harmonia Macrocosmica*, 1660. It is in the public domain because its copyright has expired.

35. The 1906 automobile calendar is by Edward Penfield, and is in the collection of the Library of Congress Prints and Photographs Division. It is in the public domain because its copyright has expired.

36. The 50-year perpetual calendar photograph is in the public domain.

37. The cartoon by John T. McCutcheon is from his 1905 collection *The Mysterious Stranger and Other Cartoons by John T. McCutcheon*. It is in the public domain because its copyright has expired.

License Description and Terms

Aside from material purely in the public domain, photographs and other material in this book are used under specific licenses permitting free use, usually with an attribution requirement. For full text and terms of these licenses, click or enter the appropriate links below. If you believe there is an error in the copyright status or attribution of any of these images, please email us.

- Creative Commons Attribution 2.0 Generic (CC-BY 2.0): http://creativecommons.org/licenses/by/2.0/deed.en
- Creative Commons Attribution-Share Alike 3.0 Generic (CC-BY-SA 3.0): http://creativecommons.org/licenses/by-sa/3.0/
- Creative Commons Attribution-Share Alike 2.5 Generic (CC-BY-SA 2.5): http://creativecommons.org/licenses/by-sa/2.5/deed.en
- Creative Commons Attribution-Share Alike 2.0 Generic (CC-BY-SA 2.0): http://creativecommons.org/licenses/by/2.0/deed.en
- Creative Commons Attribution-Share Alike 1.0 Generic (CC-BY-SA 1.0): http://creativecommons.org/licenses/by-sa/1.0/deed.en
- CC0 1.0 Universal (CC0 1.0) Public Domain Dedication (CC0 1.0) http://creativecommons.org/publicdomain/zero/1.0/deed.en
- GNU Free Documentation License (GFDL): http://en.wikipedia.org/wiki/Wikipedia:Text_of_the_GNU_Free_Documentation_License
- License Art Libre (Free Art License): http://artlibre.org

Other Books from Timespinner Press

The Story of a Special Day
Michael Dobson

A series of (eventually) 366 volumes covering everything that happened on your special day! Events, births, deaths, quotes, holidays, and much more. It's like a birthday card they'll never throw away!

US$7.95 print / US$2.99 ebook.

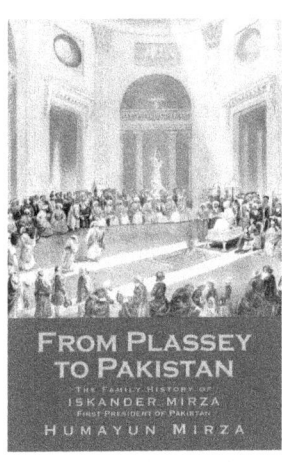

From Plassey to Pakistan
Humayun Mirza

The history of British Colonial India and the formation of Pakistan from the unique perspective of the son of Pakistan's first president and last of the royal line of Bengal, Bihar, and Orissa! This unique historical document tells the inside story of this distinguished family, including the detailed story of the coup that toppled his father from power!

US$27.95 print

A Whole New Navy: America's War in the Pacific

Miles Durr

The most comprehensive and detailed description of America's naval war in the Pacific ever—every battle, every ship, every task force and every task group from Pearl Harbor through the Japanese surrender! A must-have for the collection of every World War II buff!

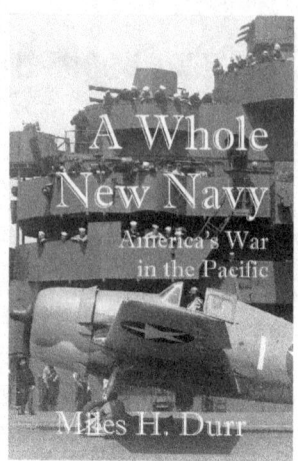

US$29.95 print

Improbable History: The Weird, the Obscure, and the Strangely Important

edited by Michael Dobson

From the birth of Western civilization to the rescue of Apollo 13, from the Leaning Tower of Pisa to Florence's Duomo, history has often turned on small, improbable details. Whatever happened to the ancient Samaritan people? Why did a fortuitous rainstorm allow the British to conquer India? How did an air raid in Italy lead to the development of chemotherapy? What happened when Albert Einstein met Adolf Hitler on the streets of Berlin? How did the Japanese manage to attack the US mainland using balloons? A cast of award-winning writers tackle some of the strangest tales in history!

US$19.95 print